DIY Dog Portraits

Featuring 8 different
art styles and more than 30
ideas to turn the love for your
pet into a work of art

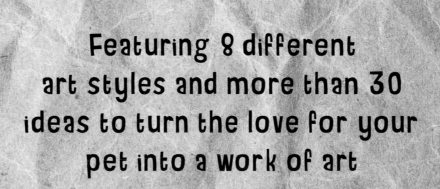

By Jessica L. Barnes, Alicia VanNoy Call, Robbin Cuddy, Jessica Ferrara, Dave Garbot,
Maritza Hernandez, Jennifer McCully, and Pauline Molinari

Quarto is the authority on a wide range of topics.
Quarto educates, entertains and enriches the lives of our readers—
enthusiasts and lovers of hands-on living.
www.quartoknows.com

Project Editor and Page Layout: Elizabeth T. Gilbert

Photo on page 8 by Maritza Hernandez, photo on page 18 by
Pauline Molinari, photos on page 28 by Jennifer Gaudet, photo on
page 54 by Samantha St. Clair, photo on page 72 by Jessica L. Barnes,
and photos on page 68 by Elizabeth T. Gilbert.
Artwork on pages 16 (bottom four images), 64 (middle, left image),
72 (middle, right and bottom two images), and all other photos
© Shutterstock.

6 Orchard Road, Suite 100
Lake Forest, CA 92630
quartoknows.com
Visit our blogs @quartoknows.com

MIX
Paper from
responsible sources
FSC® C101537

Printed in China

1 3 5 7 9 10 8 6 4 2

TABLE OF CONTENTS

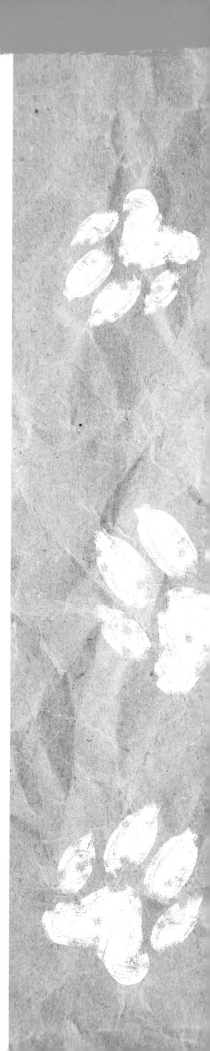

DOG BREEDS & COATS

Dog breeds range widely in size, appearance, and personality. There are more than 170 different dog breeds! As you create your pet's portrait, remember what makes your dog stand out. Is your pup tall or short? Spotted or brindle? Shy or energetic?

Standing as short as 6 inches at the shoulder, the **Chihuahua** is one of the world's smallest dog breeds.

The **Puli** has a long, corded coat that resembles a mop.

The **Sharpei** is known for its loose skin and wrinkled appearance.

The tall, skinny **Greyhound** can reach speeds of more than 30 miles per hour.

Standing as tall as 35 inches at the shoulder, the **Great Dane** is one of the world's tallest dog breeds.

DID YOU KNOW?

The height of a dog is measured from the top of its shoulder down to its feet.

Blue merle is a hair pattern that shows black markings within blue-gray hair. The markings can be spots or streaks. Dogs can also be red merle.

Roan is a hair color that shows a mix of white hairs with another color.

Fawn is a shade of brown that leans toward golden red.

Brindle is a hair pattern that shows subtle black "stripes" within another color.

Blue is a hair color that appears blue-gray.

Harlequin is a hair pattern that shows black or gray spots within white hair. These markings vary widely in size.

PAPER COLLAGE

Paper collage is an expressive,

lively, and inexpensive art form. You can use anything from old books and magazine pages to fabric and fancy scrapbooking papers!

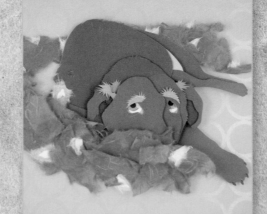

Top:
by Deon Van der Watt

Middle, left:
Tawnie by Stephanie A. Rost

Middle, right:
Toulouse by Linda Solovic

Bottom:
Jessie by Leigh Faulkner

▶ Turn the page to re-create this paper collage portrait, step by simple step!

with Maritza Hernandez

Collaging is a colorful, crafty way to capture your best friend—and it's a great way to reuse old magazines! As you work, don't be afraid to use your fingers and get messy. Also, remember that it's easy to fix mistakes in your collage: Simply cover them up with more paper!

🦴 SUPPLY LIST

- Canvas (suggested size: 9" x 12")
- Printed photo
- Ballpoint pen
- Ruler
- Pencil
- Permanent marker (fine point)
- Scissors
- Acrylic gloss medium (or decoupage glue)
- Acrylic brush (large or size 10)
- Stack of unwanted magazines
- Old towel (for protecting surfaces and cleaning)

Note: Be sure to wear old clothing!

Photo by Maritza Hernandez

REFERENCE PHOTO Begin by choosing a photo that best captures the unique traits of your pet. I chose this reference because it emphasizes the dog's wide smile and broad tongue.

STEP 1 Print your photo on a sheet of paper that works with the size of your canvas. In this project, I worked on a 9" x 12" canvas and printed out my photo in the center of an 11" x 17" sheet of paper. Once you print your photo, use a ballpoint pen to draw a 1" grid over the image.

STEP 2 Next use the pencil to create a 1" grid on your canvas, Just as you did on your photo.

STEP 3 Using your photo as a reference, draw the main outlines with pencil. Focus on each box, one by one, matching the box on the canvas to the box on your print. When finished, you will have a complete line drawing of your pet. Don't worry if your lines aren't perfect! Portraits can be abstract, realistic, or a little bit of both.

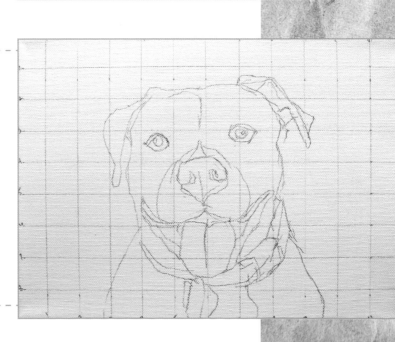

STEP 4 Now use a permanent marker to trace over your pencil marks. This helps make a bold guide for applying your bits of paper.

STEP 5 Once your marker drawing is complete, go through your magazines. Tear out the colors you need for your portrait. For this example, I tore out blues for the background along with oranges, yellows, dark browns, grays, and black for the dog. I also collected pinks for the tongue and greens for the collar!

STEP 6 Now prepare your work area by placing an old towel under your canvas. Place two cups (paper or plastic) next to your canvas. Pour water into one and acrylic gloss medium (clear glue) into the other. Now the messy fun begins! Carefully dip your brush into the acrylic gloss medium, and generously apply it to the canvas.

STEP 7 Then cut or tear the magazine pages into pieces and lay them out on the wet canvas. Don't be afraid to tear some pieces to fit very specific areas. Pay attention to the *values* (the lightness or darkness of the paper) and the colors as you apply paper bits to match the photo print. I like to start with the face and work outward.

STEP 8 As you add bits of paper, don't be shy about using plenty of acrylic gloss medium. Use this glue both under and on top of the magazine pieces to protect the paper when dry.

STEP 9 When you reach the edges of the canvas, wrap your paper bits all the way around. The goal is to cover the entire canvas so that none of the white is showing—even on the sides. If your photo print has white in it, don't leave the canvas bare in those areas. Be sure to cover them with bits of white magazine paper.

When taking **breaks** to look for the right color of paper, make sure your **brush** is sitting in water. You don't want the **glue** to dry in the **bristles** and ruin the brush!

STEP 10 Next sharpen up the details, such as the eyebrows and darkest shadows. Focus on any areas that require thin, curved pieces of paper, such as the eyes, nose, and tongue shadows. If your pet has a collar, add it now! Remember that details like this are what make your pet unique.

STEP 11 Now cover the background with the color of your choice. I used a collection of blue colors. As you do this, make sure to cover all of your permanent marker lines. At this point, your portrait will start to take shape.

STEP 12 Continue tearing and placing pieces of paper to finish the background, covering every bit of white canvas. Once all the paper is in place, you may want to stroke a final layer of acrylic gloss medium over the canvas to make sure the work is sealed.

When wet, acrylic gloss medium can appear **cloudy** and messy. Leaving your portrait alone to dry for 10 to 15 minutes allows you to see it in its true, **colorful** state. Also, remember that you can always add more details and colors later. **Take a break** from your work of art, and you might return to find it needs more work!

STEP 13 Allow the collage to dry, and watch as the colors come to life! The acrylic gloss medium will dry clear and protect the portrait. You may choose to add more layers of acrylic gloss medium for extra protection. For the final touch, add your signature in the bottom corner.

🦴 CLEANING TIPS

- Recycle any unused paper.
- Clean your brush using a bar of soap and warm water.
- Reorganize the materials for your next project.
- Thoroughly wash your hands. Acrylic gloss medium washes off with soap and warm water.

In the last century,

artists' materials have grown with technology. Computers, printers, scanners, cameras, and other machines can help you make beautiful artwork. Put them to use as you create your own modern art!

Top:
Flou-Flou by Mark Kingsley

Middle, left:
Boston Terrier by TeddyandMia

Middle, right:
Chihuahua by TeddyandMia

Bottom, left:
Dachshund by TeddyandMia

Bottom, right:
Black Labrador by TeddyandMia

▶ Turn the page to re-create this modern art portrait, step by simple step!

MODERN ART DOG

with Pauline Molinari

Use modern technology to bring Rocket the Chiweenie to life! A bright color palette and a four-canvas display give this project a twist of "pop."

🦴 SUPPLY LIST

- Printed photo of your dog (sized to fit canvas)
- Canvases (I used four 8" x 10")
- Colored cardstock
- Printer and scanner or copy machine
- Painter's tape
- Craft paint (3 to 4 colors)
- Mod Podge® or decoupage glue
- Sponge brushes
- Scissors

Photo by Pauline Molinari

REFERENCE PHOTO Choose a photo that has interesting shapes and a good amount of contrast. This pose seems to accent Rocket's triangular features, including his head, ears, and stance. Don't worry about the background in the photo—you will be cutting it away.

STEP 1 First decide how big you want your dog portrait to be based on the size of your canvas. Print out a copy of the photo. I used 8" x 10" canvases for my dog portrait, which is close to letter-sized paper, so I printed out my puppy on a simple piece of copy paper.

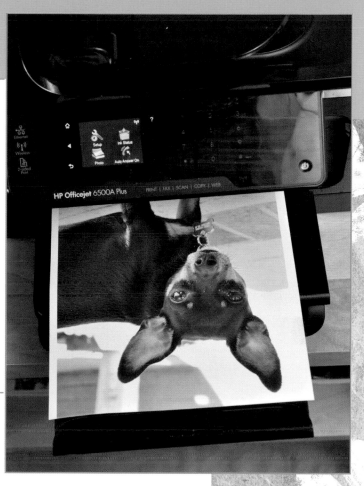

STEP 2 Use scissors to carefully cut away the background from your printed photo. You may want to cut slightly inside the outer edge of your dog to create clean lines.

STEP 3 Place the cut photo on your copier or scanner, and adjust the settings to copy the photo in black and white onto colored cardstock paper. You can play with the darkness and lightness of the copy using the settings on your copier.

STEP 4 I copied mine onto four different brightly colored papers, knowing that the black-and-white photo would stand out well on each. The result is an instant duotone effect.

STEP 5 Now use your scissors to cut away the colored paper backgrounds so that you are left with duotone photos of your puppy. Make sure your cut images fit well onto your canvases. Trim away any excess paper.

STEP 6 Now it is time to prep and color your canvases. I picked out four acrylic paint colors that match my colored paper choices, plus one more that adds a cool pop of color. Start by painting one solid layer of color on each canvas. You may need to apply two coats for full, even coverage. Allow the canvases to dry completely between coats and before moving to the next step.

🦴 MY COLOR PALETTE

Add white to your paint mixes to lighten and soften the colors.

STEP 7 Next, using painter's tape, apply random stripes from edge to edge to create six to eight smaller geometric shapes. Make sure to really press down the edges of the tape to secure it firmly to the surface, and wrap the tape all the way around the edges of the canvas.

STEP 8 Now, using the remaining paint colors, randomly fill in each of the resulting shapes. Don't worry, you can't mess this up! Again, you may need to apply one to two coats for full coverage.

STEP 9 Allow the canvas to dry before moving on to the next step.

STEP 10 When the paint is dry on your canvas, gently peel away the tape.

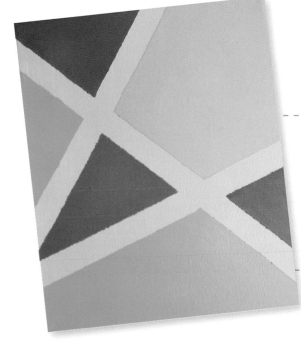

STEP 11 Now the colorful angles and shapes of your background are in place!

23

STEP 12 Prepare your Mod Podge® by pouring some into a disposable bowl. Grab a sponge brush, your painted canvas, and a cut-out print—and get ready to bring the portrait to life!

STEP 13 Apply a coat of Mod Podge on the painted canvas, place your paper dog portrait on top, and add a second coat to secure the dog. Let it dry completely. Note: The Mod Podge will appear milky, but it will dry clear.

STEP 14

When it's dry, you'll have a modern masterpiece! If you made more than one painted canvas like I did, you can hang them together in a fun Andy Warhol style!

Mod Podge is available in a variety of finishes, from **matte** to **glittery.** What matches your pooch's personality?

What's better than

a pup portrait you can cuddle and carry along with you? Learn to use a hook and yarn to create a mini version of your dog. It's easier than you might think!

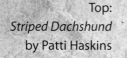

Top:
Striped Dachshund
by Patti Haskins

Middle, left:
Gus, Pug by Denise Ferguson

Middle, right:
Striped Mutt by Patti Haskins

Bottom:
Tony by Patti Haskins

▶ Turn the page to re-create this crochet portrait, step by simple step!

DIY CROCHET DACHSHUND

with Jessica Ferrara

Whether you call them Dachshunds, weiner dogs, or sausage dogs, this breed is downright adorable! Their long, unique bodies are perfect for translating to crochet.

REFERENCE PHOTOS Get a few different photographs of your dog before beginning. Take a photo from the front and from the side— the more angles, the better!

Photos by Jennifer Gaudet

SUPPLY LIST

- Worsted weight yarn, three colors (A=gray, B=turquoise, C=orange)
- G-sized crochet hook
- Yarn needle
- Polyester stuffing (poly)

NOTES

Once you understand the basic crochet stitches, you can begin your crochet project by following a pattern. Crochet patterns are written using abbreviations and terms. This pattern uses the following terms:

- Ch=chain
- Sc=single crochet
- Sc2tog=single crochet to join two stitches together

Keep in mind that this pattern is worked "in the round," which means that you will crochet each row continuously until you reach the end of the pattern. It's a good idea to mark the start of each row with a stitch marker or small safety pin.

LEARN THE SLIP KNOT AND CHAIN

STEP 1 All crochet begins with a chain. Start your chain with a slip knot. Make a loop several inches from the end of the yarn, insert the hook through the loop, and catch the tail with the end.

STEP 2 Draw the yarn through the loop on the hook.

STEP 3 After the slip knot, start your chain. Wrap the yarn over the hook (yarn over), and catch it with the hook. Draw the yarn through the loop on the hook. You have now made one chain. Repeat the process to make a row of chains.

- When counting chains, do not count the slip knot at the beginning or the loop that is on the hook.
- Use a marker to indicate the first stitch in each round.
- Leave long tails for sewing when tying off.
- Weave in yarn ends as you work so you don't have to do it all at the end.

LEARN THE SINGLE CROCHET

STEP 1 Insert the hook into the specified stitch, and wrap the yarn over the hook. Then draw the yarn through the stitch so there are two loops on the hook.

STEP 2 Wrap the yarn over the hook again, and draw the yarn through both loops. When working in single crochet, always insert the hook through both top loops of the next stitch (unless the directions specify front loop or back loop only).

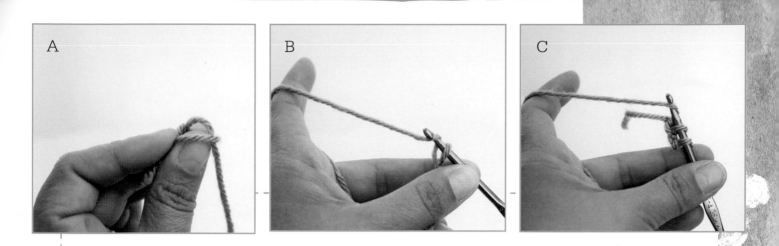

BEGIN YOUR DOG

To begin your crochet dog, make a slip knot. (See A above.)

Crochet two chain stitches (ch). (See B above.)

Crochet six single crochets (sc) in the second chain from the hook. (See C above.)

Continue crocheting in the pattern below, for each part of the dog.

Body and Head

Round 2: 2 sc in each sc around. (12)

Round 3: Sc in first, 2 sc in next. Repeat around. (18)

Round 4: Sc in first 2, 2 sc in next. Repeat around. (24)

Round 5: Sc in first 3, 2 sc in next. Repeat around. (30)

Round 6: Sc in first 4, 2 sc in next. Repeat around. (36)

Round 7: Sc in first 5, 2 sc in next. Repeat around. (42)

Round 8: Sc in first 6, 2 sc in next. Repeat around. (48)

Round 9–16: Sc in each sc around. (48)

Change to color B by laying the new color across your work and grabbing it with the hook to complete a sc. Drop the first color. After a few stitches, trim both pieces of yarn and weave in the ends. (See above, right.) Continue the pattern on the following page.

Body and Head (continued)

Round 17–20: Sc in each sc around. Change to color C. (48)

Round 21–24: Sc in each sc around. Change to color B. (48)

Round 25–28: Sc in each sc around. Change to main color. (48)

Round 29–36: Sc in each sc around. (48)

Stuff with poly fill at this point. Going forward, add stuffing every few rows as you work. (See above, left.)

Round 37: Sc in first 6, sc2tog. Repeat around. (42)

Round 38: Sc in first 5, sc2tog. Repeat around. (36)

Round 39: Sc in first 4, sc2tog. Repeat around. (30)

Round 40: Sc in first 3, sc2tog. Repeat around. (24)

Round 41: Sc in first 2, sc2tog. Repeat around. (18)

Round 42: Sc in each sc around. (18)

Round 43: Sc in first 2, 2 sc in next. Repeat around. (24)

Round 44: Sc in first 3, 2 sc in next. Repeat around. (30)

Round 45: Sc in first 4, 2 sc in next. Repeat around. (36)

Round 46: Sc in first 5, 2 sc in next. Repeat around. (42)

Round 47: Sc in first 6, 2 sc in next. Repeat around. (48)

Round 48–52: Sc in each sc around. (48)

Round 53: Sc in first 14, sc2tog. Repeat around. (45)

Round 54: Sc in first 13, sc2tog. Repeat around. (42)

Round 55: Sc in first 12, sc2tog. Repeat around. (39)

Round 56: Sc in first 11, sc2tog. Repeat around. (36)

Round 57: Sc in first 10, sc2tog. Repeat around. (33)

Round 58: Sc in first 9, sc2tog. Repeat around. (30)

Round 59: Sc in first 8, sc2tog. Repeat around. (27)

Round 60: Sc in first 7, sc2tog. Repeat around. (24)

Round 61: Sc in first 6, sc2tog. Repeat around. (21)

Round 62: Sc in each sc around. (21)

Round 63: Sc in first 5, sc2tog. Repeat around. (18)

Round 64: Sc in each sc around. (18)

Round 65: Sc in first 4, sc2tog. Repeat around. (15)

Round 66: Sc in each sc around. (15)

Round 67: Sc in first 3, sc2tog. Repeat around. (12)

Round 68: Sc in each sc around. (12)

Round 69: Sc in first 2, sc2tog. Repeat around. (9)

Round 70: Sc in each sc around. (9)

Round 71: Sc in first 1, sc2tog. Repeat around. (6)

Round 72: Sc in each sc around. (6)

Round 73: Sc2tog. Repeat around. (3)

Round 74: Sc in each sc around. (3)

Tie off, leaving a long tail for sewing.

LEGS

Ch 2 with Color A.

Round 1: 6 sc in 2nd ch from hook. (6)

Round 2: 2 sc in each sc around. (12)

Round 3: Sc in first, 2 sc in next. Repeat around. (18)

Round 4–9: Sc in each sc around. (18)

Tie off, leaving a long tail for sewing. Stuff legs lightly with poly fill. Attach front and hind sets of legs about 1" apart along the join between the main color and color B.

TAIL

Ch 2 with color B.
Round 1: 4 sc in 2nd ch from hook. (4)
Round 2: 2 sc in each sc around. (8)
Round 3–11: Sc in each sc around. (8)
Tie off, leaving a long tail for sewing. Stuff tail.
Attach at rear of body.

🦴 DID YOU KNOW?

Steel hooks are sized differently than regular hooks. The higher the number, the smaller the hook. They range from #14 or 0.9 mm (the smallest) to #00 or 2.7 mm (the largest).

NOSE

Ch 2 with color B.

Round 1: 4 sc in 2nd ch from hook. (4)

Round 2: 2 sc in each sc around. (8)

Round 3: Sc in first, 2 sc in next. Repeat around. (12)

Round 4–5: Sc in each sc around. (12)

Round 6: Sc in first ch, sc2tog next. Repeat around. (8)

Tie off. Stuff lightly, and affix to nose end of head/body piece.

EARS

Ch 5 with color C.

Round 1: Sc in first 4 ch. 2 sc in last ch. Sc in back side of remaining 4 ch. (10)

Round 2–6: Sc in each sc around. (10)

Tie off, leaving a long tail for sewing. Using a yarn needle, sew one ear to each side of the head.

EYES

Using small pieces of color B and a yarn needle, embroider eyes on each side of the head.

PERSONALIZE YOUR PUP!

Your crochet dog can be personalized with different yarn colors, button accents, safety eyes, or accessories such as a collar or leash. Also consider using a multi-color yarn or additional stripes and colors. The possibilities are truly endless!

Mixed media art combines

several different art materials in one piece. What can you combine? Just about anything! Try markers over dried watercolor. Add layers of paper. Stamp with acrylic paint. Whatever you do, make it uniquely yours!

Top, left:
Willie Jack
by Margaret Anne Suggs

Top, right:
Edmund by Kelly Saxton

Middle:
Roscoe by Rob Bynder

Bottom:
Charlie and Sam by Johanna Ochs

▶ Turn the page to re-create this mixed media portrait, step by simple step!

MIXED MEDIA SHAGGY DOG

with Jennifer McCully

In this project, give new life

to old newspaper by using it to represent the shaggy coat of a sheepdog. Combine it with paint to give your piece plenty of vibrant color and contrasting textures!

🦴 SUPPLY LIST

- Canvas, canvas panel, or wood
- Sharpened pencil and eraser
- Newspaper, cut into small strips
- Decoupage glue (matte)
- Acrylic paint
  - Two shades of blue
  - White
  - Black
  - Red
  - Green
  - Yellow
- Paintbrushes (various sizes)
- Gesso or gel medium
- Varnish (optional)

REFERENCE PHOTO
It's a good idea to choose a photo of your dog in a familiar pose. The background doesn't matter—you can change it to anything you'd like!

STEP 1 Prepare your wood panel for paint by applying two coats of gesso or gel medium. This will seal the wood so that its oils don't rot or bleed through your art over time. A coat of gesso will also smooth out the surface and provide a bright white foundation for your paint.

STEP 2 Create a vibrant background using two or three similar colors. You can also paint a solid color and then stencil over it using a different color to create a patterned or "wallpaper" look. Get creative!

STEP 3 Once the background dries, sketch out an outline of your dog. There is no need to include small details at this point, but draw where the eyes and nose will go, as these areas might not be completely covered with paper strips.

STEP 4 Cut thin strips of newspaper, and collect them near your canvas. Vary the strips in size and shape, and taper some at the ends to resemble clumps of hair.

STEP 5 Pour some Mod Podge® in a small container. Working from the inside out, brush the Mod Podge onto your canvas in sections, and cover the areas with strips while still wet. Once the strips are in place, brush Mod Podge over the strips of paper to seal them onto the canvas. Place the strips so they follow the direction of hair growth.

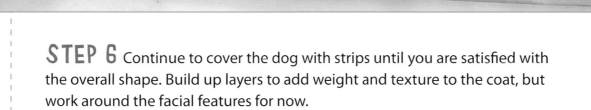

STEP 6 Continue to cover the dog with strips until you are satisfied with the overall shape. Build up layers to add weight and texture to the coat, but work around the facial features for now.

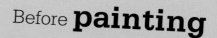

Before **painting** the facial features in the next step, it's important to let the Mod Podge dry **completely!**

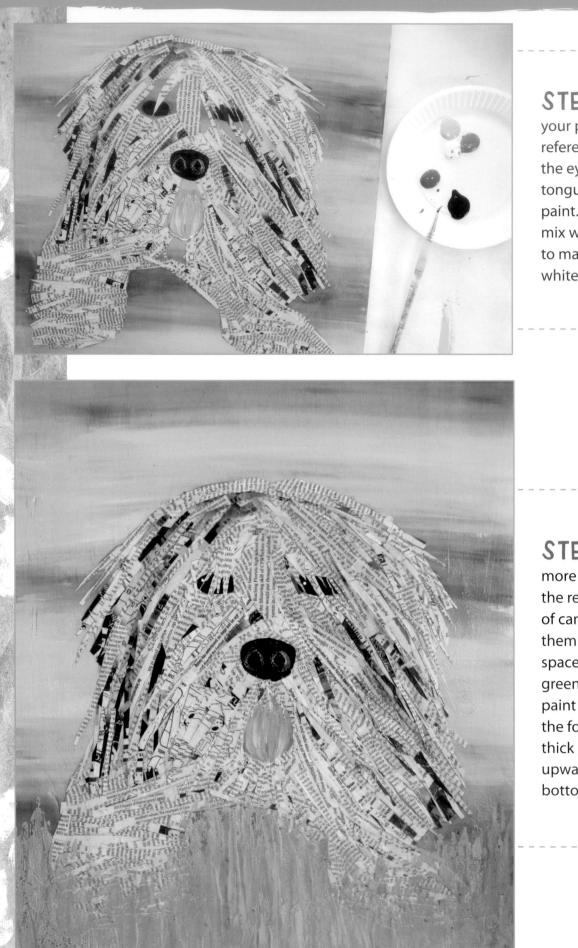

STEP 7 Using your photo for reference, paint the eyes, nose, and tongue with acrylic paint. To make gray, mix white and black; to make pink, mix white and red.

STEP 8 Now add more strips to cover the remaining areas of canvas, tearing them to fit specific spaces. Then use green and yellow paint to add grass in the foreground. Use thick paint and stroke upward from the bottom of the canvas.

STEP 9 Use white paint to add clouds to the sky and splatter on some droplets for texture. Then protect and seal your artwork by coating it with varnish. Important: Always have an adult help when working with varnish. Use spray varnish in a well ventilated area, such as outside, to avoid inhaling the toxic fumes.

CARTOONING

Cartoon pet portraits can be super cute and super silly! The trick is to highlight your pet's most noticeable feature, whether it's round eyes, a big nose, or a fluffy coat.

Top four:
Zoey
Roger
Toots
Sammy
by Marius Valdes

Bottom, left:
Fido by David Caunce

Bottom, right:
by Phil Toscano

▶ Turn the page to re-create this cartoon portrait, step by simple step!

COOL CANINE CARTOON

with Dave Garbot

Learn how to draw an accessorized hound in a playful cartoon style! This lesson breaks the drawing down into 13 very simple steps, so you can see how basic shapes and simple lines are the building blocks of any cartoon. Happy drawing!

SETTING UP Cartooning calls for just a few simple tools. It's a good idea to start your drawing in pencil, using an eraser to clean up the lines. Once you've finished the basic drawing, outline it with black marker. Then color it with markers, crayons, colored pencils, or even paint!

48

REFERENCE PHOTO Start out with a fun photo as your reference! Catch your dog in a humorous pose, or try out some accessories (if your dog is willing!). Anything goes in the cartoon world, so you can add anything you'd like to your drawing, even if it's not in the picture!

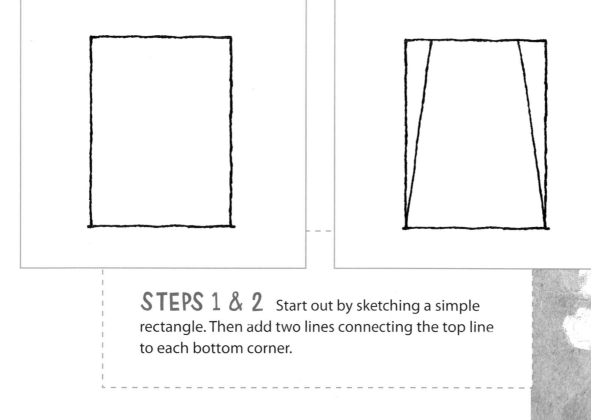

STEPS 1 & 2 Start out by sketching a simple rectangle. Then add two lines connecting the top line to each bottom corner.

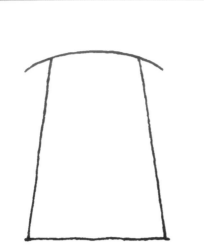

STEP 3 Add a curved line over the top to suggest the hat's bill. Erase any lines you no longer need.

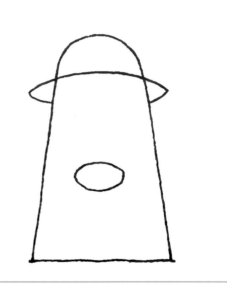

STEP 4 Add the top of the hat, and draw an oval for the nose.

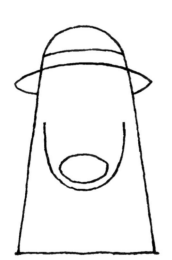

STEP 5 Add the band of the hat and a "U" shape for the muzzle.

STEP 6 Use two lines to indicate the edge of each ear. Draw the inner rims of his glasses.

STEP 7 Complete the rims of his glasses and the outlines of his ears.

STEP 8 Box in a horizontal band for the scarf.

STEP 9 Box in the remaining bit of the scarf, and outline the tongue.

STEP 10 Add a crease on the tongue, and draw the outline for each arm.

STEPS 11 & 12 Build the paws using "C" shapes, connecting four to form each side.

Remember to **have fun!** The lines don't have to be perfect. In fact, when drawing **cartoons,** squiggly lines will make your character even more interesting!

52

STEP 13 Add the final details, including speech bubbles, paw pads, a few doggy bones, and lines to show movement. Now outline your final drawing with black marker, and finish by adding bright colors!

🦴 **DETAILS**

Now that you've drawn this pup once, maybe you'd like to do it again—but a little differently next time. What if he had mittens, a different hat, or maybe even some crazy eyeballs!? Use these ideas or come up with your own.

POP ART

These modern

portraits appear to "pop" with vibrant color and plenty of contrast! Look for inspiration from famous pop artists of the past, including Andy Warhol and Roy Lichtenstein.

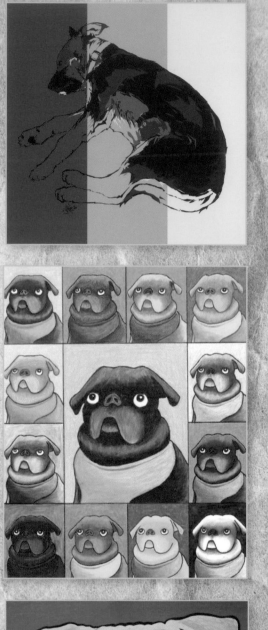

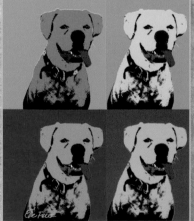

Top, left:
Charlie by Matt Lu

Top, right:
Jesse, Pit Bull by Kristin Bowen

Middle, left:
Jean-Paul, Pug by John Coughlin

Middle, right:
German Shepherd by Rami Hoballah

Bottom, left:
Lucy, Mixed Breed by R. Mike Nichols

Bottom, right:
Wilma, White Boxer by Ellie Fidler

▶ Turn the page to re-create this pop art portrait, step by simple step!

POP ART PUP

with Alicia VanNoy Call

In this acrylic project, replace the realistic colors of your photo with a funky palette and add a few fun swirls for a modern design!

🦴 SUPPLY LIST

- Stretched canvas or canvas board
- Jar of water
- Brushes (small, medium, and large)
- Paper towels
- Acrylic paint
- Mixing palette or plastic plate

🦴 MY COLOR PALETTE

- Dark purple
- Dark red
- Dark yellow
- Sky blue
- Brown
- Orange
- Light blue
- Medium blue
- Light yellow

Photo by Samantha St. Clair of Crevan Night Photography

REFERENCE PHOTO Choose a reference photo for this project. Keep in mind that this type of art works best when there is plenty of contrast (or a noticeable difference between light and dark areas).

STEP 1 Make a drawing based on your photo. (See page 68 to learn how to transfer an image.) As you create the outline, focus on the eyes, nose, and mouth—and don't forget to trace the shapes of the shadows too!

STEP 2 Build up your painting in layers, beginning with dark purple. Wet your brush, dab it on a paper towel, and then load it with acrylic paint. Use a large brush to fill in large areas of darks and shadow, and use the small brush for the thinner outlines along the ears and facial features.

STEP 3 After the purple dries, use a damp brush to apply a thin layer of light pink over the purple, including the forehead, neck, cheeks, and nose. Use this color to fill in the ears. Work loosely and don't worry about blending all the brushstrokes. Just have fun adding each layer of paint, and see what happens!

You're making a painting in colors that don't follow the rules! But for your painting to look awesome, your **values** (areas of light and dark) still need to follow the rules. Make sure the **lights and darks** in your photo are the same as the lights and darks in your painting.

STEP 4 Once the pink layer is dry, apply dark yellow around the eyes and on the cheeks using a damp brush. Don't worry about painting over the pink layer in some places; overlapping will make some interesting new colors! Let the painting dry.

STEP 5 Use sky blue to fill in the shadows of the white fur. Apply the paint thickly under the chin and over the left side of the neck. Use thinner paint within the ears and over the face.

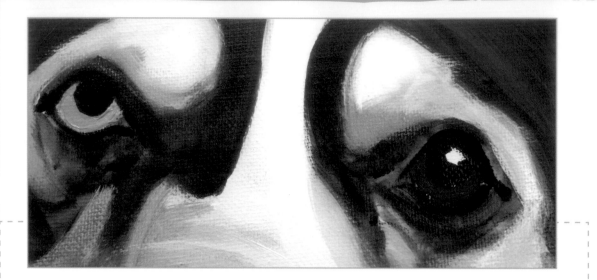

STEP 6 Working around the dark purple outline and pupil, use the small brush and thick paint to apply the first layer of each eye color. For the brown eye, apply a scooping stroke of brown paint; for the blue eye, apply a scooping stroke of light blue. Let the eye color dry.

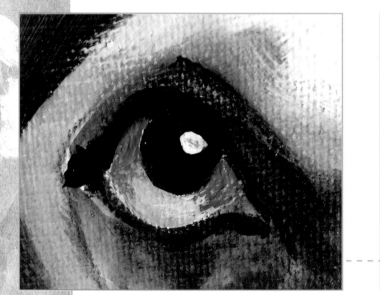 

STEP 7 Using darker versions of each eye color, paint the parts of the iris near the upper eyelids. Then add a third color to each eye using a color that is lighter than the previous two layers. (Use a light blue for the blue eye and orange for the brown eye.) Scoop this color under each pupil. Together, these three layers of color make the eye appear rounded, as though it is catching the light. To finish, define the highlight in each eye with white paint. This process of building the iris with three colors, followed by a highlight in the pupil, is the secret to realistic eyes every time!

STEP 8 Next choose any colors you want to use for the background. I chose a gradation of orange to yellow, which complements the purples of the dog. Starting in the bottom right corner, apply thick paint over the canvas. Before it dries, switch to dark yellow above the dog's head and blend the colors. As you move over the ear and down the canvas, blend into a lighter yellow.

ARTIST TIPS

- Be sure to rinse your brush thoroughly between each color.
- Acrylics are translucent, which means that light can pass through the paint. Paint in multiple layers to create deep, beautiful colors!
- Learning how to paint takes practice. Be patient—you will get better in time!

STEP 9 Paint designs in your background for a cheerful touch. I chose the light blue I used to paint the dog's eye. You can paint any designs you want: spirals, flowers, stars, or even bone shapes. If you don't want to paint them by hand, you can use a foam stamp dipped in paint.

STEP 10 Finally, with a medium brush dipped in thick paint, outline the figure of your dog. This will make the figure appear to pop out from the background. Use a small brush to create a narrow, controlled line. Create your outline in white, or use the same color as your background designs.

STEP 11 Step back and look at your painting, and add any other details you wish. Now you're done! Wasn't that fun? Remember that you can paint the same photo using a completely different set of colors for completely different results!

Colored pencil is mess-free

and inexpensive—
and you probably
have a set of pencils
at home already! Use
these colorful tools to
add simple color to
pencil drawings, or
build it up in layers
for rich colors and
textures.

Top, left:
Smokey by Dana Trent

Top, right:
Padfoot by Kim Niles

Middle, left:
Papillon by Vectoria

Middle, right:
Bulldog by Robin Cuddy

Bottom:
Scottish Terrier by Robin Cuddy

► Turn
the page to
re-create this
colored pencil
portrait, step by
simple step!

with Robbin Cuddy

The sharp tips of colored pencils make

them a great choice for a traditional, realistic portrait. It's easy to layer and blend the colors to create the look of a soft coat!

🦴 SUPPLY LIST

- Pencil
- Eraser
- Colored pencils
  - Black
  - Light pink
  - Rosy beige
  - Light umber
  - Burnt ochre
  - Sepia
  - Gray
  - Beige
  - Cream

REFERENCE PHOTO
Choose a reference photo for your portrait. It's a good idea to get a clear, full-body image so that you can zoom in and view the details at a large size. Also, remember that a dog looking straight at the camera makes an engaging portrait.

STEP 1 Use a pencil to create an outline of your dog based on the reference photo. (See page 68 for instructions on transferring an image.) Note: The outlines shown are dark so that you can see them. However, keep the outline light on your own paper so that it blends in with your colored pencil.

STEP 2 Start with a black pencil and shade the eyes, nose, and mouth. Fill in the pupils, leaving a white dot for the highlight in each eye.

STEP 3 Using the light pink and rosy beige pencils, color the tongue and the top of the nose. Fill in the iris with light umber and burnt ochre.

Photos by Elizabeth T. Gilbert

STEP 1 Print out your photo onto a sheet of paper, making it the desired size of your artwork.

STEP 2 Coat the back of the printout with a layer of graphite using a pencil. (You can also use graphite transfer paper in place of this step.)

STEP 3 Now place the printout (graphite-side down) on top of your art paper or canvas. Using a pencil or ballpoint pen, trace the outlines of your dog. Occasionally peel back the corner to make sure the lines are transferring well. The result will be a simple line drawing of your photo reference!

STEP 4 Using the light umber pencil, shape the fur by coloring all the medium tones. Stroke in the direction of the hair to create a sense of volume.

STEP 5 Begin adding beige and cream to the lightest areas of the fur. Then blend them in with light umber and burnt ochre.

There are many ways to use your colored pencils—see below for a variety of techniques that you can practice and incorporate into your drawings.

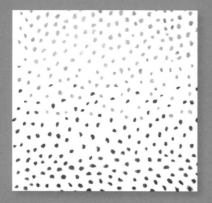

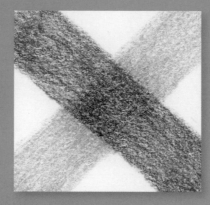

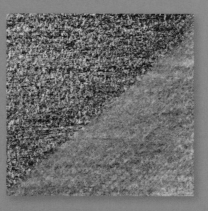

Stippling Use lots of dots to color a drawing. The more dots in an area, the darker the area will look.

Mixing Color one color over another to create a new color. In this example, magenta on blue makes purple.

Gradating Press hard to create dark strokes. As you move down the paper, don't press as hard, making the color lighter as you go.

Blending Gradate a color from dark to light. Then stroke a second color over the lighter areas of the first. You will see the colors blend together.

Burnishing To burnish, first apply a coat of your desired color. Then use a sharp white colored pencil to stroke over it at an angle. This will create a smooth, polished finish.

Crosshatching Draw straight lines next to each other. Then turn the paper and draw more straight lines over the first set. You can use this netlike pattern to fill in shadows.

STEP 6 Use the sepia pencil to color the darkest parts of the coat. Finish the paws with gray and rosy beige. Use a black pencil to add the whiskers using thin, gently curving strokes.

🦴 **DID YOU KNOW?**

A Golden Retriever's coat can range from deep red and gold to cream and white. However, the breed holds a recessive gene that occasionally yields black coats!

SILHOUETTE ART

Silhouette art starts with a simple, elegant shape. Make sure this shape captures the curves and lines that best represent your pooch. A black silhouette stands out well, but you can also use a variety of colors and patterns.

Top:
Catahoula Leopard Dog
by Acey Thompson

Middle, left:
Rooga by Misha Zadeh

Middle, right:
Puppy Dog Silhouette
by Heitor Barbosa

Bottom row:
Vintage Framed Silhouettes
by Snusmumr

► Turn the page to re-create this silhouette portrait, step by simple step!

DIY SILHOUETTE PORTRAIT

with Jessica L. Barnes

The long, sleek lines of this Labrador

Retriever are perfect for representing its alert and obedient personality. In this project, use adhesive dots to assemble a 3-D twist on classic silhouette art!

🦴 SUPPLY LIST

- Photo of dog
- White colored pencil
- Scissors
- Glue stick
- Adhesive dots (such as 3-D or Pop-Up Glue Dots®)
- 1 sheet of black cardstock
- 1 sheet of heavy chipboard (12" x 12")
- 4 sheets of colored paper (12" x 12"), including:
    - blue or sky-patterned paper
    - light green textured cardstock
    - floral-patterned paper
    - green patterned paper
- Ribbon
- Paper trimmer (optional)
- Ruler or straight edge (optional)

Photo by Jessica L. Barnes

REFERENCE PHOTO It's picture time! If you don't already have a photo of your dog, you'll need to take one. Once you get a good picture, print it out! Use either heavy cardstock or photo paper because you'll want a stiff edge for tracing (step 2). For this size project, I printed an 8" x 10" photo, and the size of the dog was about 7" tall.

STEP 1 Use scissors to cut out the dog from your photo.

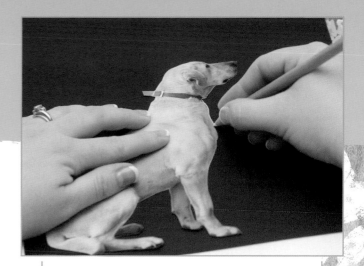

STEP 2 Using a sharp white colored pencil, trace all around the outside of the dog onto black cardstock.

STEP 3 Carefully cut just inside the white outline with scissors. Now set the silhouette aside while you prepare the background.

🦴 PHOTOGRAPHY TIPS

- Before taking any pictures, run around and play with your pup for a bit to get all the wiggles out.
- You'll want your dog to sit still for the picture, so have a few treats ready!
- Having a friend help you will make it easier—your buddy can take the picture while you tell your dog to sit and give the treats.

Formal profile shots of your dog work well for silhouette art, but don't be afraid to experiment with some **action shots** too!

STEP 4 Next attach the background to the chipboard. To prepare, take the 12" x 12" heavy chipboard and set it on your workspace. Now take the 12" x 12" blue or sky-patterned paper and smear glue all over the back of it.

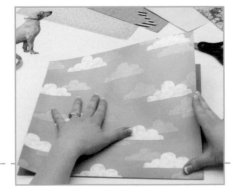

Line up the paper with the chipboard and press it down, smoothing out any air bubbles as you go.

STEP 5 Cut the 12" x 12" light green textured cardstock paper into hill shapes. I started cutting about 4 inches down. Be creative here—you can use triangular peaks for a mountainous look or rounded peaks for rolling hills.

STEP 6 Cut the 12" x12" floral patterned paper down so that it's 6" x 12". I used a paper trimmer, but you could also use scissors and a ruler to measure.

STEP 7 Now for the grass! You'll need to cut three 2" strips from the 12" x 12" green patterned paper. Using scissors, fringe-cut the strips about 1" deep (halfway), all the way across the 12" strips.

🦴 FRINGE TIP

Fluff the fringe strands so they look ruffled like grass. This will give your picture some texture and dimension!

STEP 8 Once you have all the layers ready, attach everything to the chipboard base. Place adhesive dots on the back of each layer, including the dog silhouette, spacing each dot a few inches apart.

First place the green, rolling hills over the sky, and then add the flower layer. Finish the background by adding three layers of grass.

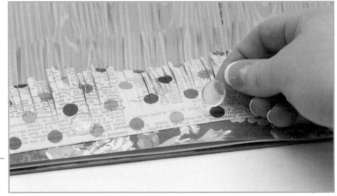

When preparing the grass layers, place the adhesive dots along the bottom, where you haven't made any cuts. Avoid gluing the fringed grass down.

STEP 9 Finish by placing the dog silhouette centered over the grass layers. Then trim any excess chipboard that may be peeking out from behind the patterned papers.

STEP 10 To display your portrait, you can either put it in a 12" x 12" frame, or you can use a ribbon to hang it, as shown in this example. Simply attach a colored ribbon to the back using adhesive dots.

STEP 11 Now enjoy your finished portrait!

MORE IDEAS!

Want to take this project to the next level? Create a glow box by assembling your layers inside of an empty tissue box! First cut off the entire tissue box top; then open up a side flap to insert your layers. To finish, use a battery-operated tea light to illuminate your layers from behind.

ABOUT THE ARTISTS

Jessica L. Barnes lives in beautiful Star Valley, Wyoming, with her best friend and husband, Daniel, and their children, Emmett and Emerson. In her free time, she runs her silhouette art shop, *www.iillume.etsy.com*. She enjoys graphic design, drawing, sewing, home improvement with her hubby, reading to her children, and listening to audiobooks.

Alicia VanNoy Call, creator of DawgArt, specializes in pet portraiture and animal art on canvas. Her paintings are inspired by the vivid colors of the desert Southwest, where she lives and works in Arizona. Alicia is an award-winning writer and illustrator and holds a BFA in illustration from Utah Valley University. Her art is found in fine retail establishments across the United States. To see more of Alicia's art, visit *www.dawgart.com*.

Robbin Cuddy began her career designing packaging for toys, games, and puzzles. She eventually became a freelance illustrator and concentrates primarily on children's books. She resides in Palm Beach Gardens, Florida.

Jessica Ferrara has a successful blog, *Chaos & Love,* and a craft room full of more supplies than she has time to use. Jessica puts her lifelong love of all things crochet to work creating patterns for everything, from quirky coffee sleeves to tween jewelry and accessories. Jessica lives in Southern California with her chef husband and two little men. For more, visit *www.chaosandlove.com*.

Dave Garbot is an experienced illustrator who enjoys working with clients to create fun and engaging images for a variety of projects. Relying on his whimsical imagination, humor, and attention to detail, Dave is often called upon for assignments in children's publishing, advertising, character development, stylish lettering, games, and fun maps. His list of clientele includes Barnes & Noble, Harper Collins, Penguin Press, Scholastic, Klutz Press, Sterling Publishing, Addison Wesley, Parenting Press, Carrabba's Restaurants, Hyatt Hotels, McDonald's, the Tribeca Film Festival, and Arnold Worldwide. For more, visit *www.garbot.com*.

Maritza Hernandez received a Bachelor's of Fine Art & Illustration at the American Academy of Art in 2006 and is currently based out of Chicago. She creates art made from collage, recycled magazines, and occasional fancy paper. She also does watercolor painting, screen printing, story boarding, oil painting, and graphic design. For more, visit *www.maritzah.com*.

Jennifer McCully is a graphic designer who expanded her horizon to include mixed media work. Her creative spirit can be seen on her bold canvases, which feature vibrant and simple objects that are energetic and inspiring. Her childlike creations evoke happiness, and her inspiration is drawn from practically anything. Jennifer is a full-time Etsy seller, operating four different shops. For more, visit *www.jennifermccully.com*.

Pauline Molinari is Editorial Director of Walter Foster Jr. and the creative magic behind the *Club Chica Circle* blog. With a long bibliography of young adult and children's titles bearing her creative talents, whether from art direction or end-to-end production, you will find Pauline's work in all major bookstore chains. Her home office is filled with pictures of her daughter, Maggie, children's books, craft projects, coloring tools, and paintings (her own). Pauline is based in Southern California, where the sun is almost always shining. Her husband, Peter, thankfully keeps her energized with Starbucks and gourmet cooking. For more, visit *www.club.chicacircle.com*.